First World War
and Army of Occupation
War Diary
France, Belgium and Germany

57 DIVISION
Headquarters, Branches and Services
Commander Royal Engineers
7 September 1915 - 29 February 1916

WO95/2969/3

The Naval & Military Press Ltd
www.nmarchive.com
Published in association with The National Archives

Published by

The Naval & Military Press Ltd

Unit 10 Ridgewood Industrial Park,

Uckfield, East Sussex,

TN22 5QE England

Tel: +44 (0) 1825 749494

www.naval-military-press.com

www.nmarchive.com

This diary has been reprinted in facsimile from the original. Any imperfections are inevitably reproduced and the quality may fall short of modern type and cartographic standards.

© **Crown Copyright**
Images reproduced by permission of The National Archives, London, England, 2015.

Contents

Document type	Place/Title	Date From	Date To
Heading	WO95/2969/3 Commander Royal Engineers		
Heading	War Diary Of 57th (West Lancs) Divisional R.E. From 1st September 1915 To 30th September 1915		
Miscellaneous	Statement		
War Diary	Ham Street	07/09/1915	07/09/1915
War Diary	Canterbury	08/09/1915	08/09/1915
War Diary	Wingham	11/09/1915	11/09/1915
Heading	War Diary Of 57th (West Lancs) Divisional R.E. From 1st October 1915 To 31st October 1915		
War Diary	Margate	07/10/1915	08/10/1915
War Diary	Ham Street	09/10/1915	10/10/1915
War Diary	Canterbury	13/10/1915	16/10/1915
War Diary	Wingham	17/10/1915	17/10/1915
War Diary	Herne Bay	18/10/1915	18/10/1915
War Diary	Bridge	24/10/1915	24/10/1915
War Diary	Maidstone	30/10/1915	30/10/1915
War Diary	Ham Street	31/10/1915	31/10/1915
Heading	War Diary Of 57th (West Lancashire) Divisional R.E. From 1st November 1915 To 30th November 1915		
War Diary	Maidstone	02/11/1915	02/11/1915
War Diary	Canterbury	09/11/1915	09/11/1915
War Diary	Bridge	10/11/1915	10/11/1915
War Diary	Wingham	10/11/1915	10/11/1915
War Diary	Ham Street	11/11/1915	13/11/1915
War Diary	Maidstone	13/11/1915	14/11/1915
War Diary	Canterbury	25/11/1915	25/11/1915
War Diary	Ham Street	26/11/1915	26/11/1915
War Diary	Brightlingsea	30/11/1915	30/11/1915
Heading	War Diary Of 57th (West Lancashire) Divisional Royal Engineers From 1st December 1915 To 30th December 1915		
War Diary	Canterbury	02/12/1915	02/12/1915
War Diary	Wingham	07/12/1915	07/12/1915
War Diary	Canterbury	07/12/1915	08/12/1915
War Diary	Wingham	09/12/1915	09/12/1915
War Diary	Canterbury	12/12/1915	23/12/1915
War Diary	Wingham	23/12/1915	23/12/1915
War Diary	Bridge	08/12/1915	21/12/1915
Heading	War Diary Of 57th (West Lancashire) Divisional Royal Engineers From 1st January 1916 To 31st January 1916		
War Diary	Wingham	02/01/1916	05/01/1916
War Diary	Canterbury	07/01/1916	30/01/1916
War Diary	Bridge	10/01/1916	28/01/1916
Heading	War Diary Of 57th (West Lancashire) Divisional R.E From 1st February 1916 To 29th February 1916		
War Diary	Canterbury	24/02/1916	24/02/1916
War Diary	Grove Ferry	25/02/1916	25/02/1916
War Diary	Littlebourne	25/02/1916	26/02/1916
War Diary	Bridge	03/02/1916	29/02/1916

WO95/2969/3
Commander Royal Engineers

CONFIDENTIAL.

WAR DIARY.
of
57th (WEST LANCS) DIVISIONAL R.E.

FROM :- 1st SEPTEMBER 1915.

TO :- 30th SEPTEMBER 1915.

LIEUT COLONEL
C.R.E. 57th (WEST LANCASHIRE) DIVISION.

"Fairbourne"
Lane John,
CANTERBURY.
2nd October, 1915.

S T A T E M E N T.

UNIT............................	57th (WEST LANCS) DIVISIONAL R.E.
DIVISION........................	57th (WEST LANCASHIRE)
TEMPORARY WAR STATION...........	KNOWSLEY PARK, PRESCOT, LANCASHIRE.
STATIONS OCCUPIED SINCE CONCENTRATION.................	Headquarters, Bessels Green, Sevenoaks,- and Canterbury.

    1/1st W.L. Field Coy R.E.- Riverhead, Kent and with Expeditionary Force.

    2/1st   - do -   Riverhead and Tonbridge, Kent ,- Oxted, Surrey,- and Wingham, Kent.

    1/2nd   - do -   Chipsted, Canterbury and Wingham, Kent ,- and with the Mediterranean Expeditionary Force.

    2/2nd   - do -   Tonbridge and Lenham, Kent,- Rye, Sussex,- and Ham Street Kent,.

    57th (W.L.)Divl Sig Coy R.E.- Bessels Green,Sevenoaks and Canterbury, Kent.

    2/1st W.L.Divl Sig Coy R.E.- Riverhead and Canterbury, Kent.

MOBILIZATION....................	Completed.
CONCENTRATION AT WAR STATION....	The concentration of 2nd Line Units at this station is still incomplete owing to the Home Service Details not yet having been replaced.
ORGANIZATION FOR DEFENCE........	Practice Alarms are being carried out by day and by night with marked improvements. The Units are however only partially armed.

Army Form C. 2118.

WAR DIARY
~~INTELLIGENCE SUMMARY~~

(Erase heading not required.)

Instructions regarding War Diaries and Intelligence Summaries are contained in F. S. Regs., Part II. and the Staff Manual respectively. Title pages will be prepared in manuscript.

Hour, Date, Place	Summary of Events and Information	Remarks and references to Appendices
SEPTEMBER.		
7th. Ham Street.	Captain A.D. Murray took over Command of the 2/2nd W.L.Field Coy R.E. From Captain L.Lomax, transferred to the 2/1st W.Lancs Field Coy R.E.	
8th. Canterbury.	The 57th (W.L.) Divl Signal Coy R.E. moved from the Hutments in the Old Park to Bridge to allow the Divisional Artillery to mobilize for service overseas. The 2nd Line 57th (W.L.)Divl Signal Coy R.E. moved from the Hutments in the Old Park to Wingham for the same purpose.	
11th. Wingham.	Eighteen Men joined the 2/1st W.L.Field Coy R.E. at Wingham., from the 3rd Line Depot, Weeton,. in part completion of Unit.	

1247 W 3299 200,000 (E) 8/14 J.B.C. & A.   Forms/C. 2118/11.

CONFIDENTIAL.
----:oOo:----

WAR DIARY.

of

57th (WEST LANCS) DIVISIONAL R.E.

FROM :- 1st October 1915.

TO :- 31st October 1915.

[signature] LIEUT COLONEL,

C. R. E. 57th (WEST LANCASHIRE) DIVISION.

"Fairbourne"
Dane John,
CANTERBURY.
6th November 1915.

Army Form C. 2118.

WAR DIARY
or
INTELLIGENCE SUMMARY.
(Erase heading not required.)

Instructions regarding War Diaries and Intelligence Summaries are contained in F. S. Regs., Part II. and the Staff Manual respectively. Title pages will be prepared in manuscript.

Hour, Date, Place		Summary of Events and Information	Remarks and references to Appendices
OCTOBER.			
7th	Margate.	1. N.C.O. 1/c of 2 Drivers and 3 horses with 2 Carts belonging to the 2/2nd W.Lancs Field Coy R.E. LEFT Margate at 9. a.m. proceeding by March Route to Ham Street, halting on the night of the 7th at Bridge.	
8th	Margate.	1 Officer with 47 Other Ranks 2/2nd W.Lancs Field Coy R.E., left Margate for Ham Street to join Unit before proceeding on Course of Pontooning at Henley-on-Thames.	
9th	Ham Street.	1 Officer and 12 Other Ranks left Ham Street for Henley-on-Thames as Advance Party.	
10th	Ham Street.	The 2/2nd West Lancs Field Coy R.E. with 5 Horses and 1 Cart proceeded from Ham Street to Henley-on-Thames for the purpose of attending a Course of Instruction in Pontooning.	
13th	Canterbury.	Five Pack Horses received by 1/1st W.L. Divl Sig Coy R.E. from Branch Veterinary Hospital, Wincheap.	
16th	Canterbury.	Eleven telegraphists transferred from 3rd Line Depot W.L.Divl Signal Coy R.E. to 2/1st W.L.L. Sig Coy R.E. in part completion of Est:	

(73989) W4141—463. 400,000. 9/14. H.&J.Ltd. Forms/C. 2118/10.

Army Form C. 2118.

WAR DIARY
or
INTELLIGENCE SUMMARY.
(Erase heading not required.)

Instructions regarding War Diaries and Intelligence Summaries are contained in F.S.Regs., Part II. and the Staff Manual respectively. Title pages will be prepared in manuscript.

Date	Hour, Date, Place	Summary of Events and Information	Remarks and references to Appendices
October.			
17th	Wingham.	Coast Defence Works, Whitstable to Birchington, handed over by 2/1st W.L.Field Coy R.E. to the 9th Provisional Brigade.	
18th.	Herne Bay.	1 Officer, 41 Other Ranks, with 8 Horses and 4 Vehicles moved by March route from Herne Bay to Monckton in connection with Coast Defence Services.	
24th.	Bridge.	Lieut E.C. Glover 57th (W.L.) Divl Sig Coy R.E. PROCEEDED from Bridge to Devonport reporting on arrival to the Embarkation Commandant there for duty with the East Anglian Divisional Signal Coy R.E.(M.E.F.)	
30th	Maidstone.	1 Officer and 6 Other Ranks arrived at Maidstone as Advance Party to 1/3rd West Lancs Field Coy R.E., who are changing stations from St Helens to Maidstone.	
31st	Ham Street.	The 2/2nd West Lancs Field Coy R.E. returned to Ham Street from Henley-on-Thames on completion of Course of Pontooning Training.	

---:ooo:---

CONFIDENTIAL.

WAR DIARY.

of

57th (WEST LANCASHIRE) DIVISIONAL R.E.

FROM :- 1st November 1915.

TO :- 30th November 1915.

"Fairbourne"
Dane John,
Canterbury.
6th December 1915.

Lieutenant Colonel
C.R.E. 57th (WEST LANCASHIRE) DIVISION.

WAR DIARY
or
INTELLIGENCE SUMMARY.
(Erase heading not required.)

Army Form C. 2118.

Instructions regarding War Diaries and Intelligence Summaries are contained in F.S. Regs., Part II. and the Staff Manual respectively. Title pages will be prepared in manuscript.

Hour, Date, Place	Summary of Events and Information	Remarks and references to Appendices
NOVEMBER. 1915.		
2nd. Maidstone.	The 1/3rd West Lancs Field Coy R.E. arrived from ST HELENS to complete the Establishment of the 57th (West Lancs) Divisional R.E.	
" "	Lieutenant C.G. Bishop, reported his arrival from the 1/2nd West Lancs Field Coy, R.E., Meditteranean Expeditionary Force., and took up duty with the 1/3rd West Lancs Field Coy R.E.	
9th. Canterbury.	Major-General A.E.Sandbach, Inspector of Royal Engineers, arrived for the purpose of Inspecting the R.E. Units of this Division.	
10th. Bridge.	Inspection by Inspector of Royal Engineers, of 57th (West Lancs) Divisional Signal Coy R.E. on a Tactical Exercise. The Inspector of R.E. stated that same was well carried out and remarked that the Unit was highly trained, they were however still incomplete in harness and saddlery, and both the technical and transport wagons. These have been indented for and are still urgently required.	

(73989) W4141—463. 400,000. 9/14. H.&J.Ltd. Forms/C. 2118/10.

2nd SHEET.

WAR DIARY
or
INTELLIGENCE SUMMARY.
(Erase heading not required.)

Army Form C. 2118.

Hour, Date, Place	Summary of Events and Information	Remarks and references to Appendices
NOVEMBER 1915. (Contd).		
10th. Wingham.	Inspection of 2/1st West Lancs Field Coy R.E., by Inspector of Royal Engineers, who stated that the Company was very much scattered and almost entirely employed on "Defence Works" which was not desirable if the Division is to be prepared for duty oversea. He also remarked that as many Officers as possible should be sent to Newark and Deganwy for the full 10 week's training.	
" "	Inspection of 2/1st West Lancs Divisional Signal Coy R.E. by Inspector of Royal Engineers, on a scheme. The I.R.E. was very well pleased with this unit and stated that the training was good.	
11th Ham Street.	Inspection of 2/2nd West Lancs Field Coy R.E. by Inspector of Royal Engineers whose remarks were similar to those of the 2/1st W.L.Field Coy R.E. The I.R.E. also remarked that the Companies should be concentrated together for the purpose of R.E. Training for War.	

3rd SHEET.

WAR DIARY
or
INTELLIGENCE SUMMARY.
(Erase heading not required.)

Army Form C. 2118.

Instructions regarding War Diaries and Intelligence Summaries are contained in F.S. Regs., Part II. and the Staff Manual respectively. Title pages will be prepared in manuscript.

Hour, Date, Place		Summary of Events and Information	Remarks and references to Appendices
NOVEMBER 1915. (Contd)			
13th.	Ham Street.	2nd Lieut A.M. Kennedy, 2/2nd West Lancs Field Coy R.E., proceeded overseas to join the 1/2nd West Lancs FieldCoy R.E., serving with the Mediterranean Expeditionary Force.	
"	Maidstone.	Advance Party 1/3rd W.L.Field Coy R.E., proceeded to Brightlingsea.	
14th	"	The 1/3rd W.L.Field Coy R.E. proceeded to Brightlingsea for the purpose of undergoing a Course in Pontooning.	
25th.	Canterbury.	Advance Party of 2/2nd W.L.Field Coy R.E., arrived for the purpose of taking over hutments for 2/2nd W.L.Field Coy R.E.	
26TH.	Ham Street.	The 2/2nd W.L.Field Coy R.E. proceeded to Canterbury by March Route from Ham Street to Old Park Canterbury on change of station, halting on the night of the 26th at WYE and completing journey on the 27th.	
30th.	Brightlingsea.	Major G.E. Oppenheim reported his arrival to take over Command of the 1/3rd W.L.Field Coy R.E.	

C O N F I D E N T I A L.

W A R   D I A R Y

of

57th (WEST LANCASHIRE) DIVISIONAL

ROYAL ENGINEERS.

FROM :- 1st DECEMBER 1915.

TO :- 30th DECEMBER 1915.

Lieutenant Colonel
C.R.E. 57th (WEST LANCASHIRE) DIVISION.

"Fairbourne"
Dane John.
Canterbury.
January 1916.

Army Form C. 2118.

WAR DIARY
INTELLIGENCE SUMMARY.
(Erase heading not required.)

Instructions regarding War Diaries and Intelligence Summaries are contained in F.S. Regs., Part II. and the Staff Manual respectively. Title pages will be prepared in manuscript.

Hour, Date, Place	Summary of Events and Information	Remarks and references to Appendices
DECEMBER 1915.		
2nd Canterbury.	Orders received for concentration of the following units as follows prior to moving to Larkhill to prepare for service with the 55th Division British Expeditionary Force :-	
	1/1st West Lancs Divl Signal Coy R.E. at Bridge.	
	2/1st West Lancs Field Coy R.E. at Whitstable.	
	2/2nd -- do -- at Canterbury.	
7th Wingham.	Advance Party arrived belonging to the 1/3rd Wessex Field Coy R.E. FROM CHRISTCHURCH.	
" Canterbury.	Advance Party, 2/3rd Wessex Field Coy R.E. arrived from TAUNTON.	
8th Canterbury.	The following moves took place :-	
	1/1st W.Lancs Divl Signal Coy R.E., Bridge to Larkhill.	
	57th (West Lancs) Divl Signal Coy R.E., Wingham to Bridge.	
	2/1st W.Lancs Field Coy R.E., Whitstable to Larkhill.	
	2/2nd -- do -- Canterbury to Larkhill.	

Army Form C. 2118.

WAR DIARY
~or~
~~INTELLIGENCE SUMMARY.~~
(Erase heading not required.)

Instructions regarding War Diaries and Intelligence Summaries are contained in F.S. Regs., Part II. and the Staff Manual respectively. Title pages will be prepared in manuscript.

Hour, Date, Place	Summary of Events and Information	Remarks and references to Appendices
DECEMBER 1915.		
9th. Wingham.	1/3rd Wessex Field Company R.E. arrived from CHRISTCHURCH.	
12th. Canterbury.	1/3rd West Lancs Field Coy R.E. arrived in the Hutments at the Old Park from Brightlingsea on completion of Pontoon Course.	
17th. Canterbury.	The G.O.C. 57th (West Lancs) Division, inspected the following Units at the places as stated against each:- 57th (W.L.) Divl Signal Coy R.E. at Bridge. 1/3rd West Lancs Field Coy R.E. at Old Park, Canterbury. 1/3rd Wessex Field Coy R.E. at Wingham. and observed that the Equipment, Boots and Picks required more attention and cleaning, also that the Companies Books were not being kept quite in order and called attention to Officers Saluting, all of these defects have now been remedied. The G.O.C. also remarked that the Horses and Mules of the Signal Coy were not in such a good condition as they should be and steps have since been taken to have these animals more properly looked after.	

(73989) W4141—463. 400,000. 9/14. H.&J.Ltd. Forms/C. 2118/10.

Army Form C. 2118.

WAR DIARY
~~INTELLIGENCE SUMMARY~~
(Erase heading not required.)

Instructions regarding War Diaries and Intelligence
Summaries are contained in F. S. Regs., Part II.
and the Staff Manual respectively. Title pages
will be prepared in manuscript.

Hour, Date, Place	Summary of Events and Information	Remarks and references to Appendices
DECEMBER 1915.		
23rd Canterbury and Wingham.	The C.R.E. 57th (WEST LANCS) DIVISION, inspected the 1/3rd West Lancs Field Coy R.E. at the Old Park, Canterbury., and the 1/3rd Wessex Field Coy R.E. at Wingham. The Companies turned out very smart and it was noticed that very strong efforts had been made to rectify the faults found by the G.O.C. at his inspection held on the 17th December.	

S.O. 354.
7 JAN 1916

Army Form C. 2118

WAR DIARY
or
INTELLIGENCE SUMMARY
(Erase heading not required.)

1st Dec 1915 to 31st Dec 1915.

Instructions regarding War Diaries and Intelligence Summaries are contained in F. S. Regs., Part II. and the Staff Manual respectively. Title Pages will be prepared in manuscript.

Place	Date	Hour	Summary of Events and Information	Remarks and references to Appendices
BRIDGE	8th	2:30 pm	The Unit moved from WINGHAM to BRIDGE. Strength 7 Officers. 225 Other ranks. 108 Animals.	P.b.
BRIDGE	9th	—	Twenty one NCO's and men were transferred to this Unit from the 1/1 West Lancs Div. Sig. Co. R.E. and taken on the Strength accordingly.	P.b.
BRIDGE	17th	11.30 am.	The G.O.C. 57" (W.L.) Divn. inspected the Unit on the BRIDGE-PATRIXBOURNE road in Column of Route. The G.O.C. was dissatisfied with the condition of the animals, fitting + cleanliness of Harness, all this has now been remedied.	P.b.
BRIDGE	21st	3 pm.	The animals of this Unit were inspected by Major Burnell A.S.R. War Office. Major Burnell rendered a satisfactory report as to condition of same.	P.b.

J. [Signature] Capt
O/c 57" (W.L.) Div. Sig. Co. R.E.

CONFIDENTIAL.

WAR DIARY
OF
57th (WEST LANCASHIRE) DIVISIONAL ROYAL ENGINEERS.

FROM. 1st January 1916. To. 31st January 1916.

[signature] Lieut Colonel
C.R.E. 57th (WEST LANCASHIRE) DIVISION.

Fairbourne.
Dane John.
Canterbury.
5th February 1916.

Army Form C. 2118.

WAR DIARY
or
INTELLIGENCE SUMMARY.
(Erase heading not required.)

Instructions regarding War Diaries and Intelligence Summaries are contained in F.S. Regs., Part II. and the Staff Manual respectively. Title pages will be prepared in manuscript.

Hour, Date, Place. JANUARY 1916.	Summary of Events and Information	Remarks and references to Appendices
2nd. Wingham.	1/3rd Wessex Field Coy R.E. proceeded to Brightlingsea for a course of Heavy Bridging and Pontooning.	
5th. Wingham.	The details of the 1/3rd Wessex Field Coy moved to the Polo Ground Canterbury.	
7th. Canterbury.	2nd Lieutenant W.Sugg, 1/3rd West Lancs Field Coy R.E. proceeded to Larkhill to join the 2/2nd West Lancs Field Coy R.E. for service overseas.	
17th. Canterbury.	The Chief Engineer, 2nd Army, Central Force inspected the R.E. Units. 1/3rd West Lancs Field Coy R.E. at the Old Park on Earthworks and Demolitions. 57th (W.L.) Divl Sig Coy R.E. on a scheme around Littlebourne and neighbourhood. 1/3rd Wessex Field Coy R.E. Rear Party of 1 Officer and 38 Other Ranks at Polo Ground, Old Park.	
21st. Canterbury.	Brig- General A.W. Roper, Inspector of R.E. accompanied by the Chief Engineer 2nd Army and the C.R.E. 57th (West Lancs) Division proceeded to the Old Park to inspect the 1/3rd W.Lancs Field Coy R.E. and to Littlebourne to inspect the 57th (W.L.) Divl Signal Coy who were carrying out a scheme. The inspector of R.E. made the following comments :- The Units were handicapped in their training owing to the deficiency of horses, harness, rifles and ammunition. The Signal Coy by the Divisional Motor Despatch Riders being used by Divisional Headquarters and therefore being away from their own unit. and the Horses and Mules of the 1/3rd Wessex Field Coy being badly groomed. The following steps have been taken to remedy the above defects :- Horses are being obtained through the Divisional Headquarters. Harness and outstanding equipment have been hastened through the D.A.D.O.S. The Motor Despatch Riders have been withdrawn from Divl Headquarters	

WAR DIARY
or
INTELLIGENCE SUMMARY.

(Erase heading not required.)

Army Form C. 2118.

- 2. -

Hour, Date, Place	Summary of Events and Information	Remarks and references to Appendices
JANUARY 1916.		
21st. Canterbury (continued)	Greater care is being taken in the grooming of all horses and Mules.	
24th. Canterbury.	1 Officer and 18 Other Ranks 2/3rd Wessex Field Coy R.E. proceeded from the Old Park Canterbury to Taunton to rejoin the Wessex Division.	
28th. Canterbury.	Lieut General Sir C.L.Woollcombe, K.C.B., G.O.C. 2nd Army C.F. inspected the 1/3rd West Lancs Field Coy R.E. during their ordinary training at the Old Park, and the 57th (W.L.) Divl Signal Coy R.E. carrying out a scheme. A deficiency of harness, horses, rifles and ammunition was commented upon.	
30th. Canterbury.	The 1/3rd Wessex Field Coy R.E. proceeded from Brightlingsea to the Old Park, Canterbury on completion of course of pontooning and heavy bridging.	

WAR DIARY
or
~~INTELLIGENCE SUMMARY~~

(Erase heading not required.)

Army Form C. 2118

From Jan 1st 1916 to Jan 31st 1916

Instructions regarding War Diaries and Intelligence Summaries are contained in F. S. Regs., Part II. and the Staff Manual respectively. Title Pages will be prepared in manuscript.

Place	Date	Hour	Summary of Events and Information	Remarks and references to Appendices
BRIDGE	10/1/16	3 pm	Lieut. V.A.C. Clay. R.E. was temporarily attached to this unit from this date by the Division Officer in Charge Signals, Drawing to assist in the training of the unit.	
BRIDGE	21/1/16	2 pm	Bdr. General Roper. Inspector General Royal Engineers inspected this unit. Bdr General Roper reported that the personnel was good & the animals well looked after.	
BRIDGE	24/1/16	11 am	Colonel Sleggett. A.D.M.S. 2nd Army Central Force inspected the billeting arrangements of the unit and reported Cook House Roof required repairing; slight draining to some billets; Old stain left behind by first line clouds to be cleaned. Steps should be taken to apply for the use of the whole of BRIDGE workhouse as billet the whole of the units therein. Steps have been taken to remedy the two former suggestion and the latter suggestion is receiving urgent attention.	
BRIDGE	28/1/16	12.30 pm	Lieut. General Sir Charles L. Woollcombe. C.B. G.O.C. 2nd Army Central Force inspected the unit whilst engaged in a Communication Scheme and expressed his satisfaction of the work then being done	

[signature] Capt.
O.C. 57. (W.L.) Div. Sig. Co. R.E.

CONFIDENTIAL.

WAR DIARY

OF

57th (WEST LANCASHIRE) DIVISIONAL R.E.

FROM :- 1st FEBRUARY 1916.

TO :- 29th FEBRUARY 1916.

_____ LIEUTENANT COLONEL

C.R.E. 57TH (WEST LANCASHIRE) DIVISION.

CANTERBURY.
6th MARCH 1916.

WAR DIARY
~~INTELLIGENCE~~ SUMMARY.
(Erase heading not required.)

Army Form C. 2118.

Instructions regarding War Diaries and Intelligence Summaries are contained in F. S. Regs., Part II. and the Staff Manual respectively. Title pages will be prepared in manuscript.

Hour, Date, Place	Summary of Events and Information	Remarks and references to Appendices
FEBRUARY 1916.		
24th. CANTERBURY.	Orders received to "Stand by" on account of possible attempted raid.	
	Orders received for a bridge to be constructed across the River Stour at Grove Ferry. This required the pontooning and bridging equipt; of both the 1/3rd West Lancs and 1/3rd Wessex Field Companies R.E. and as these two companies had no horses available for the transport of the vehicles to Grove Ferry, the bridge could not be constructed until the following day when horses were obtained from the R.G.A.	
	The deficiency of horses mentioned above is seriously hampering the training and efficiency of the Field Companies.	
25th GROVE FERRY.	The bridge was completed at 6. p.m. by a Section from 1/3rd West Lancs Field Coy R.E. and has been maintained up to date.	
" LITTLEBOURNE.	1 Officer and 20 Other Ranks, 2/3rd Wessex Field Coy R.E. arrived from Taunton, as advance Party.	
26th. "	2/3rd Wessex Field Coy R.E. arrived from Taunton.	

Army Form C. 2118

WAR DIARY
or
~~INTELLIGENCE SUMMARY~~
(Erase heading not required.)

From 1st Feb/16 to 29th Feb/16

Instructions regarding War Diaries and Intelligence Summaries are contained in F. S. Regs., Part II. and the Staff Manual respectively. Title Pages will be prepared in manuscript.

No. 9/63

Place	Date	Hour	Summary of Events and Information	Remarks and references to Appendices
BRIDGE.	3.2.16	8 p.m.	One Officer and 17 other ranks left BRIDGE to proceed to LYDD under instructions from Hdqrs. 57th (w.L.) Division.	1/1
BRIDGE	5.2.16	6 p.m.	The above party returned to BRIDGE on completion of duty.	1/1
BRIDGE	8.2.16	2 p.m.	Lieut. V.A.C. Clay. R.E. left this Unit under instructions from War Office	1/1
BRIDGE	29.2.16	2 p.m.	Major. Sir. G. Bannerman. R.E. arrived for attachment to this Unit.	1/1
BRIDGE	29.2.16	3.30 p.m.	Capt. R.C. Major Norfolk Regt. reported for attachment to this Unit.	1/1

[signature]
Capt.
O.C. 57th (W.L.) Div. Sig. Co. R.E.

www.ingramcontent.com/pod-product-compliance
Lightning Source LLC
Chambersburg PA
CBHW081507160426
43193CB00014B/2612